More Little Lessons to Live By

More Little Lessons to Live By

E. Charles Bauer

Concordia Publishing House
St. Louis   London

Quotations from the following Bible versions are by permission of the copyright holders:

Revised Standard Version, copyright © 1946 and 1952 by the Division of Christian Education of the National Council of the Churches of Christ in the U. S. A.

Today's English Version of the New Testament and Psalms, copyright © 1966 and 1970 by American Bible Society.

New American Bible, copyright © 1970 by the Confraternity of Christian Doctrine, Washington, D. C.

Concordia Publishing House, St. Louis, Missouri
Concordia Publishing House Ltd., London, E. C. 1
Copyright © 1972 by Concordia Publishing House
Library of Congress Catalog Card No. 79-185531
ISBN 0-570-03135-4

Content

Author's Preface

These little lessons were originally presented to little people. However, the response of the more mature people who "listened in" was such that it was decided to make them available to all who, in some way, might profit from them.

The language and the ideas embodied in these talks are suited to the mental level of the child. Maybe he can read them himself. Or they can be read to him. And, of course, they can be "preached" to him — the child. But the greatest Preacher of all time warned that unless we become as little children we have little chance of entering into the kingdom of heaven. Perhaps, then, it should not be surprising if in these days of intellectual sophistication these simple sermons, with a little embellishment, appeal to the sincere Christian of any age.

Moreover, these are not only *simple* sermons, but sample sermons, too. No preacher preaches successfully unless he preaches himself. In view of the current demand for material of this kind, it is hoped that these simple samples may be the seed of much more fruitful homilies as a result of the personal touch of preachers more eloquent than

THE AUTHOR

Publisher's Preface

The need for fresh and relevant expositions of the Scriptures to children wells anew continually. It is a special satisfaction therefore to be able to offer to worship leaders these pretested and popular simple addresses covering the varied themes of the Christian church year.

Rev. E. Charles Bauer knows how to speak to children. He is skilled also in conveying the lesson of a text—no matter how abstract. By means of visual illustrations the point of the Scripture lesson is made vivid and memorable, and leaders who use these talks will find the illustrations readily available or adaptable to their own setting and needs.

These 55 talks will supply the leader with a meditation for every Sunday and holiday of the church year, plus a few extra. Simple, straightforward prayers can be composed for the "congregation"—or by them—on the basis of the text and exposition. Within the seasons, the talks can be transposed to suit the local theme of the day—or they may provide the theme of the worship as they are delivered in succession.

The author's consistent accent on the child's relationship to God in Christ provides motivation and power for the life in Christ to which the hearer is led.

CHRISTMASTIDE

Reading: Isaiah 49:8-13, 22-23

Then you will know that I am the Lord; those who wait for Me shall not be put to shame. (Isaiah 49:23)

Worth Waiting For

We do not always get what we want right away. But if it is really nice when we finally get it, we say, "Well, that was worth waiting for."

In these weeks before Christmas we keep telling God that *He* is worth waiting for: "No one who waits for You shall be put to shame, O Lord." How are we *waiting* for God? Jesus tells us that "the kingdom of God is near"; and St. Paul says we should wake up "because our salvation is closer" than it used to be.

What is the big thing we are all really waiting for? Isn't it heaven? Aren't we all waiting for the day when God will come and make us happy forever in heaven? For thousands of years people waited for God to come down on earth. And finally He came on that first Christmas. When Jesus was born, they could say, "Well, He was really worth waiting for, because He is God"; and when we get to heaven we will say that was worth waiting for, too, when we see the Son of God "coming on a cloud with great power and majesty."

But we cannot just sit and *wait*—just twiddle our thumbs. We have to get *ready* for God. We have to *do* something while we are waiting. Saint Paul says we have to stop sinning and do good; and Jesus says we should stand up straight and raise our heads to Him.

11

And in one of the Bible prayers *we* say: "Your ways, O Lord, make known to me; teach me Your paths."

That is why we have Advent, to get ready for the coming of Christ — on Christmas and at the end of the world. That is why we have the purple vestments for these four weeks, to show that it is getting-ready time. Advent is not the time to celebrate and decorate. It is the time of waiting and getting ready for God by thinking about Jesus coming, by thanking God for loving us, by doing good, and by not sinning. Remember, no one who waits for the Lord shall be put to shame. If you get your heart ready for Jesus, then when you get to Christmas — and someday when you get to heaven — you will be able to say that it was really worth waiting for.

Reading: Romans 15:5-6, 9-13

Praise the Lord, all Gentiles,
Praise Him greatly, all peoples! (Romans 15:11)

Why Jesus Came

Soon you will be hearing a song which says, "Somebody is coming to town." You all know the name of that "Somebody." Of course, it's Santa Claus. But I wonder if you remember who Santa Claus *really* is. He is not just a jolly fat old man. Santa Claus is really a saint whose name was Nicholas — St. Nicholas — Santo Ni-c-o-*laus,* who is now with Jesus in heaven.

12

We get the idea of Santa Claus from good old St. Nick because he was kind and good and gave presents to people. But is Santa Claus really coming to town? Is even St. Nicholas the one we are waiting for? We are told in the Bible, "Behold, the *Lord* shall come" — not just Santa Claus, not just St. Nicholas, but God Himself is the One who is coming. Why? "The Lord shall come to *save* the nations." Jesus is coming to save us from hell, to take away our sins, to open heaven for us. That should really make us happy. That is why God says: "The Lord shall make the glory of His voice to be heard in the joy of your heart."

And what do we say when we hear this? We answer: "Stir up our hearts, O Lord, to make ready the ways of Your only-begotten Son." That is like the Advent prayer that many children say when they light the Advent candle every evening: "O Lord, help us get our hearts ready for You on Christmas." That is what we do now during Advent, we think about the coming of Jesus, not Santa Claus. St. Paul says it this way:

"Praise the Lord, all Gentiles,
Praise Him greatly, all peoples!"

Remember the reason we honor St. Nicholas — because *he* honored *God*. That's what *we* should do too: honor God with our hearts and lips, by our prayers and praises during Advent. It is all right to sing, "Santa Claus is coming to town." But it's much better to say to our Lord what St. Paul said: "I will sing praises to *Your* name."

Reading: Philippians 4:4-7

Rejoice in the Lord always; again I will say, Rejoice. (Philippians 4:4)

How to Be Happy

When I was a little boy there was a fellow in the funny papers by the name of Happy Hooligan. Happy *looked* funny because he always wore a tin can for a hat. But the funniest thing about him was that he was supposed to be happy *all* the time.

Can anybody *really* be happy *all* the time? St. Paul tells us that we should rejoice *always*. That means be happy all the time. But does it mean "have fun" all the time? You can't have fun when your tooth aches or your head aches. You can't have fun when you're supposed to go on a picnic or play baseball and it's pouring rain. But do you have to dance and sing and laugh and shout to be happy? Do you have to have a *party* in order to be happy? Is that what St. Paul means? Listen to what he says: "Rejoice *in the Lord* always."

We can never be perfectly happy all the time in this world. That is why we all want to get to heaven where we can really be perfectly happy forever. Nobody can be a Happy Hooligan, but we can all have a happy heart.

How? God tells us in the Bible: "Be happy *in the Lord;* be strong, fear not; here is our God; *He* comes to save us."

Our hearts should always be happy because Jesus *came* to save us on that first Christmas, because He *will* come to take us to heaven, and because He can *be* in our hearts *all* the time.

If! If sin does not crowd Jesus out of our heart. Sin leaves no room for our Savior and Friend. *Sin* does *not* make us happy. Do you feel real good when you curse and swear, when you get mad and fight, when you disobey and talk back? No! because that is what puts God *out* of your heart. You don't want to be a Happy Hooligan, but you do want a happy heart. Jesus will make your heart happy now and always—if you let Him in. Make up your mind now that you are going to keep sin out of your heart so our Lord will have plenty of room to come in.

Reading: Luke 1:26-38

I am the servant of the Lord. May His will for me be done. (Luke 1:38)

I Will Do His Will

Do you know what a "servant" is? Someone who "serves" somebody else. In a restaurant or large dining room servants serve your meals. A servant is someone who does something for you, who does what you want, who works for you.

Well, John ——————— works for me. You could call him my servant. He does what I want him to do.

Watch. "John, bring me the squeegee." John: "I will not!" "What did you say, John?" "I will not!" Is John doing what I want? Is he working for me? Is he serving me? Is he *really* a servant? Not as long as he says, "I will not!"

If he is really going to work for me, serve me, do what I want, what does he have to say? Yes: "I *will*." "Now, John, please be a good servant and bring me that squeegee." John: "OK, I will." "Thank you very much." (That's what this is — a squeegee.)

"I am the *servant* of the Lord. May His *will* for me be done." That is what Mary said to the angel when he asked her to be the mother of Jesus. That is what Jesus said to God the Father when He asked Him to come and save us: "I have come to do Your *will*, O God." That is what *we* should say when God asks *us* to do something: "Thy will be done."

What I want John _____ to do is called "my *will*." When he is a good servant, he says "I *will*." But if he says, "I will *not*," then he is not serving me, not working for me, not doing what I want, not "doing my *will*."

Mary was a good servant. She did God's will; she did what God wanted. Jesus is *God*. But *He* was a good Servant too. He did His Father's will; He did what God the Father wanted. That's how both Jesus and Mary got ready for the first Christmas. They both said: "I am the servant of the Lord. May His will for me be done."

That is the best way we too can get ready for Christmas. That is what Advent is for: for doing God's will. How do you *know* what God's will is? Just by listening to the people in charge of you. *They* take God's place: your parents, your teacher, your doctor, your nurse, your pastor. Every time they tell us what they want us to do, they are telling us what God's will is, what *He* wants us to do.

If you really want to be ready for the coming of Jesus, then *be* like Jesus *and* His mother. *Be* a good servant. Whenever anyone asks you to do something, just say, "I *will!*"

Reading: Isaiah 9:1-6

The people who walked in darkness have seen a great light; those who dwelt in a land of deep darkness, on them has light shined. (Isaiah 9:2)

The Real Beauty of Christmas

"All I want for Christmas is my two front teeth." I wonder how many of you remember that song? Well, it would not be very nice to be missing your two front teeth for Christmas. But did you ever think of how terrible it would be to be missing your two eyes for Christmas? So much of the beauty of Christmas comes to us through our eyes. If we could not see the burning red of these poinsettias, the refreshing green of these trees and this holly, the smile of the Babe in this crib. If we could not see the brightness of the colored lights, the glitter of the tinsel, the pretty gifts, the delicious food. If we could not see, what a difference it would make in Christmas! Yes, thank God, we have our two eyes for Christmas, because seeing makes all the difference in the world.

How terrible it would be to have all the beauties of Christmas hidden from us! How sad it would be to be in the dark; to know nothing of the brightness of God's glory; never to love the unseen things of heaven; never to be able to look upon the smile of the Babe of Bethlehem; never to know a Savior!

And that is how it was through age after age for all of God's children: all the beauties of Christmas were hidden from them, all of them were in the dark; they could not see the brightness of God's glory, and they could not love things unseen.

But, thank God, "the brightness of His glory has made itself known to the eyes of our mind by the mystery of the Word made flesh, and we are drawn to the love of things unseen through Him whom we acknowledge as God, now seen by men." Yes, that is the real beauty of Christmas: a Baby who could be seen and loved and who could show us and make us love things that we could never see or love without Him.

No wonder the apostle (Bible) tells us that this is the reason we should always and everywhere give thanks to the Lord, our holy Father, almighty and eternal God. Yes, thank God, we can now see Him with the eyes of our mind, because His Son came to be seen on Christmas. When your eyes are on Him, Christmas is really beautiful. If you keep your eyes on Him, every day will be Christmas for you. That is my Christmas wish for all of you.

Reading: Psalm 96:1-13

Sing a new song to the Lord!
Sing to the Lord, all the world!
Sing to the Lord, and praise Him! (Psalm 96:1-2)

The Gift of Faith

On your way home this morning, can you imagine stopping at some barn, throwing open the door, and seeing a newborn babe lying in the cattle's feed trough? Your first thought would be: "Somebody left their baby here." But then you notice he has not been left alone. There is a beautiful young girl and a man: it must be the proud new mother and father. But what are they doing *here* in a *barn?*

This is strange enough, but now that your eyes can see everything in the dim light of the lantern hanging there, you see other people: they must be farmers of the neighborhood. All of this is hard for you to believe. But then you notice that everyone is on his *knees*. The mother, the father, and all the farmers are *kneeling* around the baby. In fact, they seem to be praying.

What a strange sight! But suppose while you are standing there wondering, three well-dressed men come into the barn with precious gifts and fall on their knees before the child. And finally, you just can't believe it, but the place is flooded with light and you see the cowstalls filled with adoring angels!

Remember, I am asking you to imagine that this

happens to you on your way home — let us say on your own road — at the farm next door.

It couldn't! You say it could *not* happen. But it *did*. It did happen on the first Christmas. And it has been happening ever since: angels and men, princes and paupers, young and old for nearly two thousand years have sung the words "O come, let us adore Him" and have fallen on their knees before a little Baby.

If there is any kind of being everyone can love, it is surely a little infant. It does not surprise us to see someone hugging and kissing a little child. But the whole world on its knees before a Baby in a stable, that is impossible — unless you believe, believe that the Child is *God*. Then it is easy to fall on your knees before Him.

It has never really seemed strange to us to see Mary and Joseph, angels and shepherds, Wise Men and kings on their knees around the Christ Child. Why? Because we have the gift of faith. All the Christmas presents in the world could never equal this gift which God has given us. Thank God this Christmas Day that it seems so natural to you to fall on your knees at the sight of His Son. Thank God for the gift which makes it so easy for you to sing, "O come, let us adore Him, Christ the Lord."

And sorrow, like a sharp sword, will break your own heart. (Luke 2:35)

How to Accept Disappointments

Today I want you to use your imagination. I want you to make believe. Make believe that you are a little tiny baby again. This is just a doll. But let's suppose it is you. Your mother and father have just brought you to church to be baptized and afterwards I take you in my arms. Then I say to your mother, "This kid is going to make a *lot* of trouble for you." How would your mother feel? Pretty bad. And when the trouble came, she would feel even worse!

Well, something like that happened to Mary when Jesus was a little baby. Today's Bible story tells us how Mary and Joseph took the baby Jesus to church. There they met an old man who held the Child in his arms and told Mary that she would have a lot of trouble because of Him. And the trouble started right away.

Even while our Lord was still a baby, you know, King Herod tried to kill Him. And then you remember how people later on were always arguing with Him and trying to catch Him. And, of course, they finally did kill Him by hanging Him on the cross. So Mary really had a lot of trouble because of Jesus.

What did she do? Complain and scream, curse and

swear? You can't even *imagine* Mary doing any of those things, can you? Did she get all excited and upset? No, she didn't do that either. Remember, Mary had trouble right from the start—trouble finding a place for her Child to be born. And where was He born? In a barn, because no one would let them in. That was Christmas. But it was a "silent night," a "holy night," and all was calm and bright because Mary knew how to take trouble. And, of course, it was her Son Jesus who helped her to take her troubles without cursing or hollering, without screaming or swearing.

That is the lesson we have to learn from Jesus and Mary. When things go wrong, how do you act—like Mary, or like a wild animal? Remember, things were silent and holy, calm and bright because *Jesus* and *Mary* were that way—no matter how much trouble they had. Jesus will help us to be that way too. So when things go wrong, don't *you* go wrong. Act like "yon Virgin Mother and Child."

Reading: Luke 2:15-20

The shepherds went back, singing praises to God for all they had heard and seen; it had been just as the angel had told them. (Luke 2:20)

The Bright Side

Something that is very easy for all of us to do is to complain. When things don't go the way we want them to, we mumble and grumble and sigh and cry. "I don't like this and I don't like that; this is all wrong and that is no good and something else is terrible." Those are things that we say all the time. But do we stop to think about the good things? Do we remember the wonderful things? Do we look at the bright side of the picture?

You have all heard the song which tells us to count our blessings. Well, that is just what the church tells us to do today. Our worship starts right out today by saying: "Sing to the Lord a new song." Why *sing* to the Lord? Because "He has done wondrous deeds." And what are the wonderful things the Lord has done? The Gospel tells us: "All the ends of the earth have seen the victory of our God." (Ps. 98:3)

Some people say they didn't get very much for Christmas, or they don't like what they got, or it isn't what they wanted. They forget that we *all* got something very wonderful for Christmas. They forget that the best Christmas present of all came from God. They forget what the very first words of today's liturgy tell us: "A Child is born to us, a Son is given to us." God gave us Jesus for Christmas. And Jesus brought us heaven for Christmas. That's why the prayer says, "Sing joyfully to God, all you lands." Everybody has plenty to be thankful for, because God Himself came down from heaven on Christmas so we could all go up to heaven someday. Is there any *better* Christmas present than that? Could anyone ever give us a better gift than God and heaven? Aren't those the blessings we really should count? Isn't that the best reason in the world to sing and shout for joy?

I saw a sign once that said "kwitcherbeliaken."
That's a funny way of saying "stop complaining." The
best way to start this new year is to stop complaining.
All of us mumbled and grumbled and cried and sighed
plenty during the past year. Did that make us *happy?*
If you want to be happy, you have to "kwitcherbeliaken." I hope you will start right now to count your
blessings, think of the good things, remember that
God gave us Jesus for Christmas and that Jesus will
give us heaven someday. Please remember that all
this year, because I would like you to have a *happy*
new year!

Reading: Psalm 72

All the kings will bow down before Him; all nations
will serve Him! (Psalm 72:11)

Let Everybody Serve Him!

When you look into the crib at Christmastime,
you see everyone down on his knees: first of all Mary
and Joseph, then angels and shepherds, and now the
three Wise Men. They are all on their knees in front
of a little Baby, because they really believe that the
Baby is God.

You and I also get down on our knees at the crib.
And we kneel down for the same reason—because we
really believe that the Christ Child is God. But what
happens when we get off our knees? What happens

24

when we leave the crib? Do we keep on showing that we really believe?

I wonder what the Wise Men did after they left Jesus. I wonder if they forgot all about Him. They came a long, long way to find the Christ Child, so I'm sure they didn't just forget Him after they left. If the Wise Men were really wise, they would keep on showing that they believed in God.

We cannot stay on our knees all the time. But getting on our knees is only one way of honoring God. Some people are not able to kneel down at all, but that does not mean that they don't believe in God. Today we pray that everyone should honor God by giving Him gifts, by singing to Him, and be getting down on their knees. This is how we remember that "all nations will *serve* Him."

That is how we really show that we believe in God, that is how we really honor Him and show that we love Him—by doing what He wants.

The gold and frankincense and myrrh of the Wise Men would not mean a thing to the Christ Child if they did not give Him their hearts. Getting on their knees would be nothing if they would not obey God.

Kneeling down and telling God all kinds of nice things will not do us any good, either, unless we are ready to *serve* Him. Tell the Christ Child today that you are going to be a "wise" man too. Tell Him that you are going to prove that you believe in Him and love Him by always trying to do what He wants.

Reading: Luke 2:41-52

So Jesus went back with them to Nazareth, where He was obedient to them. (Luke 2:51)

Doing as We Are Told

Come with me for a few minutes to a little place called Nazareth. On the corner is a little house with a shop in the back yard. A little Boy is playing in the yard. His mother is in the kitchen cooking, and her husband is working in the shop. The Boy's name is Jesus. His mother's name is Mary, and her husband's name is Joseph.

If you watch these people for a while, you will see that they are very nice people. They never fight or get mad. They never curse or swear. They do not lie or steal.

But besides that, they help one another. They pray together, and they are very happy. If you watch the little Boy, you will see that He always does what Mary and Joseph tell Him to do, and He does it right away.

And who is the little Boy? We said His name is Jesus. And, of course, you know Jesus is God. Imagine—God is doing what He is told, God is minding Mary and Joseph, God is obeying people!

Now, you know that God is above everybody. God is in charge of everything. God made everything. God made everybody. He made Mary and Joseph. Does God have to mind anybody, then? Does He have to do what

Mary and Joseph want Him to do? No! He does not *have* to, but He *wants* to. Jesus *wanted* to obey, He *wanted* to do as He was told.

Why? Why did God put Himself under the people He had made? Why did He want someone in charge of Him? He did that to show us how to live. He obeyed to show us how to obey. Jesus did as He was told because He wants us to do as we are told.

When the Gospel tells us that Jesus "was obedient" to Mary and Joseph, it means that God let Mary and Joseph have charge of Him and He minded them. God puts people in charge of *us* too, and He wants *us* to mind them.

Can you imagine Jesus misbehaving, talking back to Mary and Joseph, or not minding them? Even though He is God, Jesus always obeyed and did what He was told. That's what He wants you to do, too. Think of that Holy Family in Nazareth. Try to behave like Jesus. Ask Jesus to help you.

Reading: Psalm 97

The Lord is King! Be glad, earth! Rejoice, all you islands of the seas! . . . all the gods bow down before Him. The people of Zion are glad, and the cities of Judah rejoice. (Psalm 97:1, 7, 8)

Adore God!

If you met a great football player right after he had won a big game, or a wonderful singer after a beautiful show, or the strong man in a circus who had just lifted a thousand pounds, I wonder what you would do. Would you put out your hand and say, "What did you bring me?" or, "Gimme a nickel," or, "How much do I get out of it"? I hope not! When we meet a hero, we shake hands, pat him on the back, congratulate him, tell him what a great game he played or what a wonderful show it was. When someone has done a good job, we praise him, honor him, tell him something nice.

Or think of your friends. Do you show people you like them by "getting" something from them all the time? You show that you like others by giving them things, by doing things for them, by saying nice things to them.

That is what we should remember also about God. In church God's messengers keep reminding us to "adore God," to "declare the works of the Lord." They keep saying, "The Lord is King! Be glad, earth!" "The right hand of the Lord has struck with power." And they keep showing us that Jesus is God, that He is all-powerful, powerful enough to change water into wine, to heal all kinds of sickness, to do all kinds of miracles, greater things than all the heroes of the world can do.

Because God is the greatest, the strongest, the most wonderful, the most beautiful, the most powerful, we should "adore" Him. We have something more to do than tell Him our troubles. We should tell Him how great He is, how wonderful He is, how powerful He is. We should praise Him, honor Him, worship Him.

We do that when we come to church, when we kneel down, when we bow our heads, when we fold our hands, when we sing, when we say, "Glory to God in the highest," "Holy, holy, holy," and, "Hallowed be Thy name." These are some of the things we do and say to show God that we think He is "the Greatest."

Reading: Matthew 13:24-30

One night, when everyone was asleep, an enemy came and sowed weeds among the wheat, and went away. (Matthew 13:25)

Enemy at Work

You have heard people say, "It's growing like a weed." They say that because weeds grow big and fast. If you plant a nice garden and take really good care of it, it will still have some weeds in it. But if somebody who doesn't like you comes along when you are not looking and *plants* weeds in it, then you will have a whole garden full of weeds.

Now let us suppose that our soul is a garden. St. Paul tells us what we should plant in the garden of our soul: the beautiful flowers of kindness and goodness and love—just like the farmer in today's Gospel planted a beautiful field of wheat. But what happened? Someone who hated the farmer came along and planted weeds in his field. Does anything like that ever happen to the garden of our soul?

29

Weeds are *bad* things. People do not want them in their gardens or their wheat fields because they spoil them and choke out the good things. What would the weeds of your soul be? Sin and bad habits. No matter how careful you are, some sins and bad habits are liable to get into your soul. But what if someone hates you and really tries to put those bad things into your soul? Do you think anyone ever tries to do that? Oh, yes, there is someone who is always trying to plant the weeds of sin in your heart: your enemy, the devil.

Did you notice when the farmer's enemy planted the weeds in his wheat field? "When everyone was asleep," the story says. And that is what the devil also tries to do—he tries to catch us asleep. When? At night, after we go to bed? No, he tries to catch our *soul* asleep. Our soul is asleep when we are not praying, not staying close to God, not on the lookout for trouble. When we are lazy and wasting time and not doing anything, when we go around with bad people and don't get away from things that are bad for us, that's when the devil comes along with his bad seeds. He won't be able to plant them in *your* soul, though, if you listen to St. Paul: " . . . whatever you do, do everything in the name of the Lord Jesus." If you do everything in the name of Jesus, you will never be near trouble and danger, and the devil will not catch you sleeping.

Reading: Matthew 13:31-35

I will use parables when I speak to them, I will tell
them things unknown since the creation of the world.
(Matthew 13:35)

Christ Our Teacher

Did you ever go swimming on the bottom of the
ocean? I never did. But I have seen some of the things
that are down on the ocean floor. Maybe you have
too — even though you can't swim. We have seen some
of the secrets of the seas because other men have taken
pictures of them. A camera can show us a lot of things
that we would never know about otherwise.

If I asked you why God came down on earth, why
Jesus was born, I wonder what you would say. I think
most of you would say that He came so He could die
on the cross for us. That's right! But Jesus came for
other reasons too. I wonder if you know some of those
reasons: to give us grace, to show us how to be good —
and He came to *teach* us, to tell us things we never
knew before.

If somebody didn't take a camera down to the floor
of the ocean, you could never see what is there — could
you? — because you cannot get down there by yourself.
All the beautiful fish and plants and shells would be
hidden from you.

That's the way it would be if Jesus never came to
teach us. A lot of beautiful things we know about God
and heaven would be hidden from us unless Jesus told

them to us. We would not know how to get to heaven if Jesus didn't teach us how. And how do we know what Jesus said? By listening to our pastor and church teachers.

The big thing Jesus came to do was to die for our sins. But that isn't all—He came to teach us, too. On Sundays the big thing we come to church for is to offer our praise to God. But that isn't all we come for—we come to learn what Jesus taught. That's why we have a sermon in church. That's why I am preaching to you now.

If we want to get to heaven, it isn't enough just to pray to God. We have to *know* about God, too. That is why we should listen to the sermon on Sunday. When we come to church, we should pay attention to what the pastor does, but we should also listen to what he *says,* because he tells us what Jesus taught—and Jesus taught us how to get to heaven.

LENTENTIDE

My grace is all you need; for My power is strongest when you are weak. (2 Corinthians 12:9)

We Need God's Help

I have here a beautiful plant. You know that this plant needs light and heat and water. You know what will happen if you keep it in the dark, put it out in the cold, or don't give it any water.

Of course, the *plant* does *not* know. Now, just let us suppose the plant could talk. Listen: "I don't want any water; I am going out in the snow; what good does it do to stay in the sunlight?"

What would you say? "It keeps you alive—that's what good the sunlight does. If you don't have water and keep warm, you will die." Our Lord said something like that when He told us that seeds planted out in the road or on top of a rock or in a bunch of thorns are not going to amount to much, because they are not going to get what they need to make them grow.

You see, the seeds cannot make themselves grow, the plant cannot keep *itself* alive. They need certain things to make them grow and to keep them alive. So do we: we need heat and light and water, too. We need food and drink and a lot of other things to make us grow and keep us alive. We would be as stupid as this plant if we said, "What good does it do to eat and drink and keep warm?"

Well, do you know that some people say things

just as stupid as that? Some people say, "What good does it do to go to church? Why do I have to pray? Why do I have to go to Communion? What good does it do? Why do we need it?"

Why do we need it? Because we are weak. So we need God's grace and strength to keep our souls alive and make them grow. Just as seeds and plants and our own bodies cannot get anywhere without food and drink and light and heat, so our souls cannot stay alive by themselves. They need the Word and the sacraments because they are weak.

St. Paul tells us in today's reading that being weak is nothing to be ashamed of. He says, "Look how weak I am; but see how much I can do when I let God help me." Let's face it: every one of us is weak, but God will make us strong if we let Him help us through His Word and sacraments.

Remember, this plant could not be strong and beautiful—could not even live—without heat and light and water. You and I cannot live without God, either. But with Him we can live a good life here and everlasting life in heaven.

Reading: Luke 18:31-43

Jesus asked him, "What do you want Me to do for you?" "Sir," he answered, "I want to see again." (Luke 18:40-41)

What Do You Want Most?

If you could have anything you wanted right now, I wonder what you would take. Would you say, "I want a million dollars," or, "I want to be the prettiest girl in the world," or, "I want to be a king and live in a beautiful palace with a hundred servants"? Or would you be like the blind man in today's Gospel story and say, "I want to see again"?

Oh, if only we could see! If only we could see what is best for us! If only we could see what we really need! If only we could see what we really should ask for! If we could see the truth, we would not ask for palaces or beauty or money. St. Paul tells us that everything else is no good without the one thing that really counts. He tells us what we should want most of all, the thing that really matters: love.

Our Lord Himself told us the same thing. The two big commandments, He said, are to love God and our neighbor. He was always preaching the law of love. And many times He showed His love for His people by helping them as He did the blind man today. And today too Jesus tells us that He is really going to prove His love for us by suffering and dying for us. That is how much God loves us.

And how much do we love Him? Do we love Him enough to suffer and die for Him? Can we really say that we love God as much as we should? Can we say that we love God's people as much as we should? I guess not! If we had as much love for God and our neighbor as we should, would we complain, would we act the way we do, would we hate and fight and not care about others? I guess not! So what we really need is love. I think our Lord and St. Paul know what they are talking about: they tell us that everything else will be fine if we just have enough of it. So the best thing to ask for is love. Remember to ask the Holy Spirit to fill your heart with it.

Reading: Matthew 17:1-8

So they looked up and saw no one else except Jesus. (Matthew 17:8)

Keep Your Eye on Jesus

That is all Jesus wants *us* to do—just see *Him*. If you had to look at just *me* all the time, that would be terrible; you would get sick and tired of seeing no one but me. Is it that way with "seeing" only Jesus with the eyes of your soul?

Well, suppose you are hungry and I say, "Sorry, I can't give you anything but food." Or suppose you are cold and I say, "Sorry, I can't give you anything but heat." That wouldn't make sense, would it? Food is what you want when you're hungry. You don't want to go dancing or swimming when you're starving – you want to eat! And when you're freezing, you don't want an ice cream cone – you want a heater!

We have been talking about keeping our eye on God, about looking to heaven. If we see only Jesus with our hearts, will we get sick and tired of Him? You don't get hungry because you're eating; you don't get cold because you're standing by the fire. Why do you get hungry? Because you do *not* have food. You get cold because you do *not* have heat. I could give you everything in the world but food and it wouldn't keep you from getting hungry.

It's something like that with our souls too. Our souls are cold without Jesus. Even if we have everything else in the world, our souls will still be hungry and cold without Jesus. And that's what we do, isn't it? We have our eye on everything but Jesus. We have our eye on having a good time, on having our own way, on doing as we please. And so we forget Jesus. Does that make us happy? No! It leaves our souls hungry and cold.

Now during Lent we think about getting our eyes off those other things so we will see "no one else except Jesus." Getting other things out of our way helps us to see Jesus better, and the better we see Jesus, the better our soul will be. Jesus is God, and God is everything. When we see Jesus, we see everything that's good for us, everything our soul needs to keep from getting cold and hungry, everything our soul needs to get to heaven.

Tell Jesus that you are going to try to get your eye off doing as you please, having your own way, just thinking of fun. Tell Him you are going to try to give up the things that make your heart blind so you will be able to see only Jesus. All you need to keep warm is heat; all you need to keep from being hungry is food. All you need to get to heaven is Jesus.

Reading: Mark 9:2-8

Peter spoke up and said to Jesus: "Teacher, it is a good thing that we are here." (Mark 9:5)

Pay Attention to God

Achtung! Sorry, I did not mean to scare you. But I did want to wake you up, to make you pay attention. And that is exactly what that word means. "Achtung" is the German word for "pay attention" or "listen to me." Well, I suppose you are going to say, "But I *was* listening to you!" With your ears, yes. But were you listening with your heart—were you really paying attention?

I wonder how many of you have noticed anything different up here today. Not many of you, I guess. (Show light bulb.) But now you all see it, don't you? This bulb was here all the time, but you did not *notice* it until I lighted it. You are paying attention to it now—but you weren't before it was lighted.

Something like that happened in the story which today's Gospel tells us. Jesus went up a mountain with three of His best friends. There His face got as bright as the sun and His clothes were all lighted up. He really looked like God, and you can bet those three friends of His paid attention to Him. In fact, Peter said, "Teacher, it is a good thing that we are here." Peter and those other two apostles were with Jesus all the time, but they were not saying "It is good that we are here" all the time. They saw Jesus every day, but they did not always pay attention to Him. But when Jesus is "transfigured before them," they really "sit up and take notice." Now they really see that Jesus is God.

And that is what this service is for: to make us sit up and take notice, to make us pay attention to God. We come to church often; we pray every day; we hear sermons every Sunday. But do we always remember that we are in God's house, that we are talking to God, and that we are listening to God's Word?

Lent should be like saying *Achtung!* It should be like turning on the light. It should help us pay attention to God. It should help us remember that church is God's house, that we come to talk to God, to listen to God, and to say to Him, "Teacher it is a *good* thing that we are here!"

Reading: Ephesians 5:1-9

Since you are God's dear children, you must try to be like Him. Your life must be controlled by love, just as Christ loved us and gave His life for us as a sweet-smelling offering and sacrifice which pleases God. (Ephesians 5:1-2)

Imitate God by Loving

"Yes" and "no" are very little words, but they are words which mean great big things. It can be very good or very bad to say no. Let's think of your best friend's birthday. It would be good to say, "No, I'm not going to hurt Joe today because it's his birthday," but it would be much better to say, "Yes, I'm going to say 'Happy Birthday' to Joe today." Now, if Joe is really your best friend, you will do something more than that, won't you? You will *give* him something to show how much you think of him: a present or a cake or a party.

Again today our Lord and St. Paul both tell us how important it is to say no to the devil, to temptation, and to sin. And they both tell us how important it is to say yes to God: Jesus says that the ones who are really happy are the ones "who hear the Word of God and keep it"; and St. Paul tells us to "follow the way of love." It is good to say no especially to sin. It is good to say yes, too, by loving God and doing what He wants.

You know that the big thing God asks us to do is to love—to love God and people. We show our love for God and His people by saying yes to Him and no to the devil. We say yes when we *tell* God we love Him or when we say we love His people, when we pray, go to church, behave ourselves. But there is another way to say yes, too; another way to show God and our neighbor that we love them—and that is by *giving*.

St. Paul says today that our Lord showed His love for us by *giving* Himself for us. Jesus showed how much He loves us by giving up His life for us on the cross and by giving His body and blood to us in Holy Communion.

Millions of people do not have enough to eat, do not have clothes to wear or a house to live in. We can show that we love those people, and God too, by *giving* them something. Every year we have a collection for people poorer then ourselves. It's a chance for you to *give* something—even if it is only a penny—to help the poor people of the world. Please say no to a candy bar or something this week and use the money you save to say yes in the collection. Remember, giving is part of saying yes; it is part of loving. Be sure to bring a quarter, a dime, a nickel, or even a penny for the collection so you can say a real loud yes.

Reading: John 6:1-15

There is a boy here who has five loaves of barley bread and two fish. But what good are they for all these people? (John 6:9)

Help for the Poor

I guess this would be almost the smallest loaf of bread you have ever seen. Now, suppose all of you were hungry and I said, "Well, I have a loaf of bread." I am sure you would say the very same thing that Andrew said to our Lord: "But what good are they for all these people?" Well, you know what the answer of Jesus was: He fed over five thousand people with five little loaves of bread not much bigger than this.

Today there are many, many more than five thousand people who are hungry. Over half the people in the world do not have enough to eat — or drink or wear. Surely we cannot feed them with a little bread. Jesus could do that because He is God. But you and I cannot do miracles.

Now, I want to show you something else very small, so small most of you cannot see it. It is the smallest piece of money we have: a penny. Think of the millions of people who need shoes and shirts, slippers and skirts. Surely we cannot buy all the things they need with a penny. What good is that for so many?

Watch! I am going to put my penny into this jar. Then I will add one for every one of you. You see, the jar is full. There are three hundred pennies in the jar now. And that is not just pennies—that is three *dollars.* I can buy ten *big* loaves of bread with three dollars. Of course that will not feed all the hungry people in the world. But, you see, we can help a lot more of them *together* than we can by ourselves. On this Sunday every year people all over the world put their pennies, nickles, dimes, and dollars together to help all the poor people who have no money, no clothes, no food, no place to live. Remember, even one penny that you give will help them.

And it will help you too. One of the best things we can do for ourselves is to help others, to show love for our neighbor. It is one of the things God wants us to do all the time, not only for a special collection. Even if we do not have a *penny,* we can help other people by praying for them. And everybody can do that. Today we are praying for the poor people of the world. Please give them a penny or a nickel or a dime if you can. But *pray* for them every day. Your prayers will help them. And *helping* them will help *you.*

Reading: John 8:46-59

They picked up stones to throw at Him; but Jesus hid Himself and left the temple. (John 8:59)

Don't Say No to Jesus

That little word "no" is a word which usually hurts. It even hurts us to say no to the things we like

45

when we should not have them. But, of course, *that* is the idea; saying no is *supposed* to hurt. But the word "no" can hurt when I ask if you like me. It hurts if someone says, "No, you may not go to the movies." It hurts a fellow when the girl he asks for a date says no; and it hurts a girl when we say, "No, your new dress is not pretty."

Now just think for a minute how it must hurt our Lord when people say no to Him. The more you love someone, the harder it is when he says no to you. Well, God loves all of His people more than they can ever understand. But how often those people of His say no to Him! Every single sin is a no to God. Every time we break one of God's laws, we turn against Him and say no to our best Friend.

When Jesus was on earth, His people were always saying no to Him. Especially in the weeks before He was put to death, they were against Jesus over and over again. They argued with our Lord and kept telling Him He was crazy — until they finally picked up rocks to throw at Him. And of course you know how it ended: on Good Friday with the biggest no the world has ever heard, when His enemies hung Jesus on the cross.

Every single suffering of Jesus came from that awful word "no." It was an awful word because it was said by people He loved so much, and His sufferings all came from that word, because every whip, every thorn, every nail means, "No, we do not believe You, we do not trust You, we do not love You, we will not serve You."

Think of all the times those people said no to our Lord. Think of how much it hurt Him because He loved them so much. He loves us just as much. Think of all the times we have said no to Him—every time we have sinned, it has been like a nail or a thorn or a whip which has said, "No, I do not believe, I do not trust, I do not love, I will not serve You!" How much longer are we going to keep on saying no to our best Friend?

EASTERTIDE

Reading: Psalm 118:15-24

What a wonderful day the Lord has given us; let us be happy, let us celebrate! (Psalm 118:24)

Stay on the Side of Jesus

Today everyone is happy. Three days ago everyone was sad. On Friday we felt bad because our sins had made Jesus die on the cross. Now, why are we so happy today? Everyone can tell me: because it is Easter — because Jesus came back to life today. But why does that make us so glad?

On Good Friday, when our Lord was dying on the cross, He did not look like God. The people who hated Him seemed to be winning, and Jesus seemed to be losing. But who was winning on Easter Sunday? Jesus. When our Lord came back to life, He showed that He is really God, because only God could raise Himself up from the dead. He showed that He had won the fight against death and sin and the people who hated Him.

That's what Easter shows us: that Jesus is God and the winner. That's the first reason why we are happy today.

But there is another reason, too. You know we are all going to die. Someday we will be dead and buried. Will that be the end of us? Oh, no! Our souls go right on living. Only our bodies are buried. But they won't stay buried. Our Lord told us that we too will rise from the dead; that our bodies and souls will come back together; that we will come to life again just as He did on Easter Sunday.

And that's the second thing that Easter shows us — that we too will someday be the winners. We will win the fight over death and sin and the devil who hates us, IF we stay on our Lord's side.

When you are here, you are on our Lord's side. That's a big reason to be happy. I hope you are having a happy Easter today. And I hope you will always stay on the side of Jesus, so you will always be happy — right on into heaven.

Reading: John 20:19-31

Jesus came and stood among them. "Peace be with you," He said. (John 20:19)

Peace Is Up to You and Me

I would like you to help me do the preaching this morning. First of all, I want to see how quiet you can be: not a sound, please. Sh-h-h. Now, listen: Could you hear that? It was a pin (amplified): so quiet you could hear a pin drop. Now, I would like you to do something else: everyone, please talk — say something to the one next to you, anything, but say it out loud.

Stop! You saw what I dropped this time: another "pin," but a great big rolling pin. And you could not hear it. Why? Because there was too much noise. And who was making the noise? You! *You* can make it noisy—or you can make it quiet and peaceful.

You heard the first word Jesus said on the night He came back to life: "Peace," the same word that was said on the night He was born. We say it every Sunday: "Glory to God in the highest, and on earth *peace* . . . ." And we pray every day for peace on earth. But there *is* no peace on this earth. Instead of kindness we have fighting. Instead of love we have hate. And who is doing the hating and fighting, who is making the noise of war? People. People like you and me. The same people who could make peace and quiet, who could be kind and loving.

You and I are not making war. But we are just like the people who are. We are people who can be kind and loving, who can make peace and quiet. But *are* we, do we? Ask yourself: When was the last time I had a scrap with another boy or girl, cursed and swore, called names? How long since I shouted, hollered, talked back to someone in charge? Who was the last one to make trouble in my house? Now, be sure you are honest when you answer those questions.

Our Lord came down from heaven to bring us peace. He lived and died to give it to us. He came back to life to make sure we would have it. But we can spoil it if we want to—just as we can spoil the quiet in this church. Jesus *gives* us peace. Let's keep it, not throw it away.

Reading: John 10:11-16

I must bring them too; they will listen to My voice.
(John 10:16)

Be a Good Sheep

Some people are afraid of dogs and cats because
they might bite or scratch. Everybody is afraid of
lions and tigers because they kill. But who is afraid
of a lamb or a sheep? A lamb might run away from *you,*
but you would never run away from a lamb, because
lambs and sheep never bite or scratch or kill. But
they are often killed by other animals because they
are weak and do not know how to fight back. That is
why they have to have someone to take care of them
and watch out for them. Other animals are always trying to kill them, so they need a good shepherd to pro-
tect them.

You and I are like sheep. The devil is always
trying to kill us. He is not afraid of us. He tries to
kill our souls with sin. And we are like lambs and
sheep because we are weak and do not know how to
fight the devil by ourselves.

When a wolf comes to kill the sheep, the shepherd
has to fight for them; he has to chase the wolf away
because the sheep are not able to. We need someone
to fight for us too; we need someone to chase the devil
away because we are not able to.

If the sheep are going to stay alive, they have to
have a good shepherd to take care of them. If our souls

are going to stay alive, we have to have a good shepherd to take care of us too. Jesus is our Good Shepherd. He is strong enough to fight the devil because He is God; and He knows how to chase the devil away, because He is God.

This is what Jesus tells us today: He is our Good Shepherd; He knows that we need His help; He will never go away and forget us; He loves us enough to die for us; He wants to help everybody, even those who do not know Him and love Him.

If Jesus is such a Good Shepherd, then we should be good sheep. *Let* Him help you, *stay* close to Him so He can take care of you, *try* to know Him better and love Him more, do *not* run away from Him, *thank* Him for dying for you. If you are always in the arms of the Good Shepherd, you will never end up in the claws of the wicked devil.

Reading: John 16:16-22

In a little while you will not see Me, and then a little while later you will see Me. (John 16:19)

Trust in the Lord

You have all seen magicians. They pull rabbits out of empty hats and grab things out of the air. (Pull a rabbit out of a hat.) Sometimes they show you something and all of a sudden it's gone. Then it's there again. "Now you see it, now you don't" is what some of them say.

Our Lord sounds like that (doesn't He?) when He says first, "You will not see Me," and then, "You will see Me." So, would you say our Lord is a magician? No! Magicians fool us and play tricks on us. But Jesus does not do that. Jesus is God and can do wonderful things without fooling us or playing tricks. When He says something, we know we can trust Him because He would never try to put anything "over" on us.

This is what we call "hope." When our Lord says that we will see Him again, we know He is not fooling. We know we will see Him in heaven someday because He promised us we would. But, of course, He promised that to those who love Him and follow Him.

We all know of course that it is not easy to follow Jesus. We need God's help if we are going to do that. But He promised us that too when He said, "Ask, and you shall receive." So we can trust God to help us.

But sometimes we are bad, anyhow. If we sin, we cannot get to heaven unless our sins are taken away. And Jesus promised to take away our sins when He said: "He who believes in Me and is baptized shall be saved." So we can trust God to forgive us.

It should make us happy that God has promised us forgiveness and help and heaven. Our Lord wanted to make us happy when He said: "In a little while you will not see Me." He wasn't fooling us. We should tell Him many times that we trust Him, that we have hope in Him. Just say, "Jesus, I know You will help me; I know You will forgive me; I know I will see You —in a little while."

Reading: James 1:17-21

Submit to God, and accept the Word that He plants in your hearts, which is able to save you. (James 1:21)

Welcome the Word of God

When I went to school, I used to pass by a high stone wall every day, and I always wondered what was on the other side. Some of my friends used to tell me that there were beautiful gardens behind that wall, filled with all kinds of wonderful flowers. Then one day the boy who lived on the other side of the wall asked me if I would like to see his father's gardens and took me through the gate. What a beautiful sight! I never saw so many pretty flowers.

Our Lord is like that boy. He shows us His Father's beautiful gardens. Many friends of ours used to tell us about God and heaven. We call them the prophets. But then Jesus, God's own Son, came to give us a really good look. He really showed us what God and heaven are like. He showed us how to live, how to be good, and how to get to heaven.

And that is just what our Lord does every Sunday morning in the liturgy. In the Epistle and Gospel and homily or sermon we hear the Word of God. It is just like being let into God's beautiful garden to see and smell all the wonderful flowers of heaven.

How lucky we are that Jesus has come to show us all about God and heaven! So "sing to the Lord a new song; for the Lord has done wondrous deeds."

"Welcome the Word of God because it has power to save your souls," and "the Spirit of truth will guide you along the way of all truth."

When we come together to listen to the Word of God in church, we are not wasting our time. If we pay attention and think about what we hear, it will make us better children of God. God's Word is the key to heaven. It will let us through the gate where we can really see and smell all the wonderful flowers in our Father's garden.

Reading: John 16:22-30

For the Father Himself loves you. He loves you because you love Me and have believed that I came from God. (John 16:27)

God Takes Care of Us

The song says, "I ain't got nobody — and nobody cares for me." We all feel like that sometimes: Some days you think the whole world is mad at you and nobody cares whether you are dead or alive.

Well, even if the whole *world* is mad at you, there is Someone who cares whether you are dead or alive — and that's *why* you are alive, because Someone is keeping you alive, and He is keeping you alive because He cares, because He *loves* you.

Sometimes we think a person does not love us because he does not give us what we want. Now, suppose a father has a shiny knife in his hand. His little boy wants the knife, but he will not give it to the baby. Is that because he does *not* love the child? No—he won't give him the knife because he knows it will hurt his little boy, and he doesn't want him to get hurt because he *loves* him. Even though the baby cries and gets angry, his father will not give him the knife because he knows what is best for his child.

You are the little boy. God is your Father. God loves you very much, and He knows what is best for you. Suppose you ask God for something. Should He give it to you if He knows it will hurt you? Would God really love you if He gave you something that would be *bad* for you? No, of course not.

But God does *love* you—He loves you so much He does not want you to get hurt. He knows that some things you will want hurt you—especially your soul—so He will not give you those things.

When we ask God's help, we are asking our best friend. He will always help us because He loves us; but He does not always give us what we want because He knows it will hurt us, it will be bad for us.

When you ask God for something, remember that. He loves you. He gives you only what is good for you. You should never turn against God because He keeps something away from you that is harmful. He does it because He loves you.

PENTECOSTTIDE

Reading: Ephesians 1:17-23

I ask that your minds may be opened to see His light, so that you will know what is the hope to which He has called you, how rich are the wonderful blessings He promises His people. (Ephesians 1:18)

Ever Ever Land

When somebody we like goes away, we always feel bad. And if we know that we are never going to see a good friend of ours again, we feel even worse. So the friends of our Lord must have felt terrible when they saw Him going up into the clouds on Ascension Day, because He was their best Friend, and it looked as if they were never going to see Him again.

But we know that Ascension Thursday is not a day to feel sad. It is a day to feel *glad.* That is why we say: "All you people, clap your hands, shout to God with cries of gladness." And the angels told the friends of Jesus the reason for being glad: "This Jesus who has been taken away from you up to heaven will come back in the same way that you saw Him go." It always makes us feel better when we know that our friend is coming back. And we know that our Lord *is* coming back someday, at the end of the world.

Besides that, we know something even better. We know why Jesus went back to heaven: to "sit at the right hand of God the Father," as we say in the Apostles' Creed, to be the King of heaven and earth. And we know something still better, something that our

Lord Himself told us: that He was going to go back to heaven to get a place ready for us there. And that is the best thing of all, isn't it? Jesus came down to earth on Christmas to get rid of the death of sin by dying on Good Friday for us. He came back to life on Easter to show that we too will come back to life after we die. And now He goes up to heaven on Ascension Day as a promise that we will someday have life forever and ever.

The life that God came to bring us is not just ordinary, everyday life. It is the life of God Himself, the life of heaven. That is what we learn when we read: "He was taken up into heaven, that He might give us a share in His divinity."

God came down on earth so He could be like us. Now He goes to heaven so we can be like Him.

Is it any wonder that the psalm says, "God mounts His throne amid shouts of joy"? Is it any wonder that it says, "All you people, clap your hands, shout to God with cries of gladness"? Is it any wonder that we are happy to see Jesus going back to heaven, when we know He is going to make a place ready there for us so we can really be happy—forever and ever?

Reading: John 14:18-24

I will not leave you alone; I will come back to you. In a little while the world will see Me no more, but you will see Me. (John 14:18-19)

Gone but Still Here

What is black and white and read all over? Right! A newspaper. We call that a riddle because it is hard to figure out and because it sounds funny. Well, do you know that Jesus gave us some riddles too? Yes, our Lord said some funny things that were hard to figure out. You just heard one of His riddles — "the world will see Me no more, but you will see Me." Even the apostles called that a riddle and kept wondering what it meant; they couldn't figure it out.

When you know that the black and white thing is not *colored* red, but that it is read by people who *read* it, then you can understand why it is a newspaper; then it makes sense to you. "But you will see Me" makes sense to you when you know that Jesus went back to heaven on Ascension Thursday and that He will come again at the end of the world. Our Lord *told* His apostles the answer to that riddle.

But, believe it or not, there is more to the riddle: "I will not leave you alone." That is like saying, "I am going away, but I am really not going away." And that is exactly what Jesus meant. He really did not go away from us. His earthly body went up to heaven, yes. He will not walk in here this morning and sit down next to you so that you can see Him. He will not use His hands to give you His body and blood in Holy Communion. It was not His voice which spoke the words of God to you today.

All this is true, but it does not mean that God has gone away and forgotten us, that Jesus is not near us, that we are back here on earth and our Lord is way off somewhere in heaven, millions of miles away — like the "man in the moon."

How many times we hear: "The Lord be with you"! Those are not just empty words, because the Lord *can* be with us, the Lord *is* with us — as long as *we* are with Him. It is never Jesus who goes away from us. *We* are the ones who do the going away. As long as we love God and our neighbor, we are with God — and He is with us. When we lose love, we lose God. Sin means not loving God; sin means not *having* God. When you love God and God's people, the Lord is with you. That is what we mean when we say: "Hear, O Lord, the sound of my call . . . . Of You my heart speaks; You my glance seeks; Your presence, O Lord, I seek. Hide not Your face from me."

God will never hide His face from you as long as you do not hide from Him. He will not leave you orphans if you do not leave Him. Remember that every time you hear, "The Lord be with you."

Reading: Acts 2:1-11

Then they saw what looked like tongues of fire spreading out; and each person there was touched by a tongue. They were all filled with the Holy Spirit. (Acts 2:3-4)

A Heart Full of Love

This is a bottle of Cola. In this other bottle is poison. The Cola bottle is filled right to the top. Can I put some of the poison in the Cola? No, because the bottle is already full of Cola and there is no room for anything else. If I want to put poison into the Cola, what do I have to do? Right, I have to take some of the Cola out. You see, there is no room in this bottle for anything bad as long as it is filled with something good.

That is exactly how it is with our hearts. If they are filled with something good, there will be no room for anything bad. Today we hear over and over again about the Holy Spirit "filling" things. The opening prayer says that the "Spirit of the Lord has filled the whole world." In the reading we heard that "a sound from heaven filled the whole house," and the people "were all filled with the Holy Spirit." And we pray: "Come, Holy Spirit, fill the hearts of the faithful." We want the Holy Spirit to fill our hearts. With what?

Well, the rest of the prayer answers: "and kindle in them the fire of Your love." That's what our hearts should be filled with, the love of God. That's what

Jesus tells us today too: "If anyone love Me . . . My Father will love him, and My Father and I will come to him and live with him."

If our hearts are filled with the love of God, do you think there will be room in them for bad thoughts, for lies, for hating, for cursing and swearing. If our hearts are full of love, will fighting and talking back and disobeying and stealing be able to get into them? But these bad things *do* get into our hearts, don't they? That is because they are not filled with something good. There is room in our hearts for sin because they are not all filled up with the love of God.

The Holy Spirit can really fill our hearts with that love if we *let* Him. And He really will if we *ask* Him to. That's the only way we can keep sin out of our hearts—by making sure they are full of love. Make sure that your heart is by saying over and over: "Come, Holy Spirit, fill my heart with love."

Reading: Matthew 28:18-20

Go, then, to all peoples everywhere and make them My disciples: baptize them in the name of the Father and of the Son and of the Holy Spirit. (Matthew 28:19)

Holy Trinity, Make Us Holy

I have three tapers here, and I am going to light one of them. Now just suppose this is our heavenly

Father. You know He sent His Son, Jesus, to save the world. So I will light the second taper from the first. That shows Jesus, the Light of the world, coming from His Father in heaven. Now we have God the Father and God the Son. Well, after Jesus had saved us by dying on the cross and coming back to life here on earth, you know He went back to the Father in heaven: so the two flames are together again. And that is when the Father and the Son sent the Holy Spirit into the world to fill men's hearts with the fire of love. So I light the third taper from the first two and we have three burning tapers that make us think of the Father, the Son, and the Holy Spirit.

But are there *three* Gods? "No," you say, "only one." That's right! See what happens when I put all three tapers together—*one* flame. But there are still three tapers, just as there are three *Persons* in God, which makes us say, "Blessed be the Holy Trinity." And the one flame shows us that there is only *one God,* which makes us bless the "undivided unity." We are honoring *the unity,* or oneness, of God and the trinity, or threeness, of the Persons in God.

Isn't it wonderful that we have a heavenly Father to take care of this big family of His? Isn't it wonderful that our heavenly Father sent His Son to save us? And isn't it wonderful that the Father and the Son sent the Holy Spirit to fill us with love?

No wonder we bless the Holy Trinity. No wonder we sing and say, "Holy, holy, holy," because we have such a holy Spirit in our hearts. That surely should make *us* holy. And that's the way we become when we really belong to God's family. As we bless the Holy Trinity, may the Holy Trinity bless us and keep us holy in the name of the Father and of the Son and of the Holy Spirit.

SUNDAYS
OF THE YEAR

Hurry out to the streets and alleys of the town, and bring back the poor, the crippled, the blind, and the lame. (Luke 14:21)

Everyone Needs God's Help

Splash! You just fell into the lake and you can't swim! What would you do? Holler for help, of course. If you were caught in a burning building, what would you do? The same thing — you would shout, "Help!" from the bottom of your lungs. If we were drowning or burning to death, we would surely need help, we all know that. But some people think that they do not need much help outside of that.

In the story which Jesus tells, the man who puts on the big dinner is God. And the house which He wants filled is the church in this world and heaven in the next. And who are the ones who come to the dinner? The poor and the crippled, the blind and the lame. They are the ones who belong to God's family, the ones who are in God's house. That means you and me.

Now, poor and crippled people, blind and lame people need help. How many times all of us help others who have no money, no food, no clothes. How many times we help those who cannot walk or cannot see where they are going. Well, all of us have been crippled by sin and blinded by the devil. All of us are poor and lame when it comes to doing good. All of us stumble and lose our way sometimes on the road to heaven.

Yes, in God's house every one of us is poor and crippled, blind and lame. So we need help.

The Word of God tells us this over and over: "The Lord came to my support. He set me free in the open and rescued me. — In my distress I called to the Lord, and He answered me. — O Lord my God, in You I take refuge; save me from all my pursuers and rescue me. — Return, O Lord, save my life." All of these mean that we need help and that God is the One to give us the help we need.

One of the first prayers we say in church every Sunday is, "Lord, have mercy," and one of the last is, "Lamb of God, have mercy on us." "Have mercy on us" means "help us." Some people seem to think that they can get along without God's help. If you ever feel that way, just remember how poor and crippled, how blind and lame all of us are when it comes to being good and staying on the road to heaven. When you remember that, you can see why we ask God to have mercy on us ever so many times.

Reading: 1 John 3:11-18

Our love should not be just words and talk; it must be true love, which shows itself in action. (1 John 3:18)

Love One Another

Did anyone ever give you a slap or a punch or a kick? Did anyone ever curse or swear at you or call you names? Did anyone ever steal from you or give you a hard time? That happens to everybody, doesn't it? But who are the people who do the things that hurt you? They are your neighbors. And Jesus says we have to love our neighbor. Do you have to love the people who hit you and curse you and hurt you? Yes! That is what Jesus wants you to do.

But how can you love people who do things you don't like? That's the difference right there! Jesus does not tell us we have to *like* being kicked or called names. You don't have to *like* the thief who steals your nice new sweater or your good radio. We can't *like* everybody, but we can *love* everybody.

Now, how in the world can you do that? How can you *love* somebody you don't like? When you love somebody, you don't want anything bad to happen to him, you want him to be happy and have good luck. You would never wish anything bad on your best friend. That is what love means—just wishing good to somebody else. Can you wish *good* to somebody you don't *like?*

Just think of Jesus for a minute, hanging on the cross. Did He *like* that? Did it make Him feel good to have those nails in His hands and feet and that crown of thorns on His head? Was He happy when the people went by and laughed at Him? Did He really *like* those people? Of course not! But did He wish bad things on them? No, He didn't do that either. He *prayed* for them; He asked His Father to *forgive* them; He wished good to them because He loved them.

That is what we have to do. That is what St. John

is telling us—that we should show in deeds that our love is real. We have to *do* the right thing toward everybody, even when they do things we don't like, even when we don't like the people themselves. No matter what they do, we still want to *love* them, and the best way to do that is to *forgive* them and *pray* for them. That's what Jesus did. That's what we should do.

Reading: Psalm 9

Sing praise to the Lord, who rules in Zion! . . . God remembers those who suffer; He does not forget their cry. (Psalm 9:11-12)

Our Heavenly
and Earthly Father

"Get lost" might be what you say to some people sometimes. But can you imagine your father saying that to you? A good father never wants his children to get lost. In fact, if a child does get lost, the first one to go looking for him is his father. And a good father will do everything to find his lost child. That is the way God has made fathers. He made them to love and watch over and take care of their children. And that is why we love our fathers and obey them and pray for them and why we have Father's Day.

Now, why do you suppose God made fathers that

way? He made them that way because He is a Father too; because He is the Father of all of us, our heavenly Father. And the prayers today tell us what our heavenly Father is like. In the first prayer we say to our Father in heaven: "Look toward me, and have pity on me, for I am alone. . . . Put an end to my . . . suffering, and take away all my sins." We ask God to help us, because we know He is a good Father. Then in the second prayer we tell God that He does help us by watching over us: "O God, You are the Protector of all who trust in You."

St. Peter tells you that you *can* trust your heavenly Father "because it is He who takes care of you," and the psalmist says, "When I called upon the Lord, He heard my voice." And our Lord Himself tells us that He is like a good shepherd who leaves all his sheep to go looking for one that is lost. Our heavenly Father does *not* want us to "get lost," and if we do, He does everything to find us.

The Holy Writings tell us to sing praise to the Lord because He never forgets us when we are in trouble. No good father ever forgets his children when they are in trouble. That is why God has told us to honor our earthly fathers. When we honor our fathers on earth, we honor our Father in heaven, because He is the Protector of all and has given us our earthly fathers to help us on our way from earth to heaven. May our heavenly Father bless our earthly fathers, and may we honor both of them so that none of us may ever "get lost."

Reading: Psalm 27

The Lord is my Light and my Salvation; whom should I fear? (Psalm 27:1)

You Can Count on God

Did you ever go fishing and sit there and sit there and sit there and never catch a thing? You know what we say when a fisherman doesn't catch anything: he was just drowning worms. And that is pretty discouraging. No fisherman goes fishing just to drown worms; he goes to catch fish.

Well, Peter and his friends were not fishing with worms; they were fishing with nets — all night long — and they never caught a single fish. They must have felt pretty bad, especially because those fellows made their living by fishing. Now can you imagine how they felt when Jesus told them to throw their nets into the water again? They said, "What's the use? There just aren't any fish here today." But you know what happened then? Our Lord fixed things so that they caught a whole load of fish. They caught so many fish they couldn't believe it.

Peter and his friends were ashamed. They felt terrible because they had not trusted Jesus. It was a good lesson for those men: they learned that God never lets people down and that they could always trust in Him.

That's a good lesson for us too, isn't it? How many times we get into trouble and then just throw up our hands and say, "What's the use?" How many times we "take it out" on somebody else because somebody doesn't come to see us or write us a letter! How many times we get all upset and "fly off the handle" because somebody scolds us or swears at us or lies about us!

But what did Jesus teach His disciples, and what does He teach us today? Jesus showed His friends that they should trust in Him. When they trust in Him, they say what the psalmist prayed: "The Lord is my Light and my Salvation; whom should I fear? The Lord is my life's Refuge; of whom should I be afraid? . . . My foes and my enemies themselves stumble and fall. Though an army encamp against me, my heart will not fear."

If I am on God's side, nobody can really hurt me; if God is with me, it doesn't matter who is against me; if I trust in God, I have nothing to fear and nobody to be afraid of. As long as I am God's friend, even a whole army cannot really hurt me. That is the lesson we should learn today. Remember that lesson with this little prayer: "Lord, You love me — I trust You."

Reading: 1 Peter 3:8-15

You must all have the same thoughts and the same
feelings; love one another as brothers, and be kind
and humble with one another. (1 Peter 3:8)

Remember,
You Are God's Family

"Mama!" That is the first word most people learn
to say — and "Daddy" is usually the second one. Just a
month ago everyone was telling us how much we
should love "Mama" — on Mother's Day. And today it
is "Daddy" who gets all the praise, because it is
Father's Day. But everybody knows that we don't
love our mothers just on Mother's Day and our fathers
only on Father's Day. All of us should love our parents
every day, and we should always show that we love
them. I hope that all of you are saying prayers for
your fathers today — but I hope that you pray for your
father *every* day.

Now, how about our heavenly Father? We are
supposed to love Him more than anybody else. He is
God, and we must love God above all things. When?
Just on Sunday — because it is the "Lord's Day"? Well,
that would be like loving your earthly father just
today — because it is Father's Day. Now, you don't
write your father a "love letter" every day. You don't
call your mother on the phone every ten minutes and
tell her that you love her. And we don't have to keep

telling our heavenly Father that we love Him every minute either. In fact, it isn't what we *say* that shows people we love them as much as what we do.

And that's exactly the way it is with God. God is our heavenly Father, and we are all His children, members of His family, brothers and sisters. And it is the way we treat the rest of God's children that really shows how much we love God. That's why Jesus says: If you want to show your love for God, make sure that everything is OK with God's people first. If you have a gift for your heavenly Father, be sure that you are friendly with your earthly brother. Don't try to give God anything until you can give love to your neighbor. If you are not on good terms with God's family, then you cannot be on good terms with the Father of the family.

St. Peter said it this way: "You must all have the same thoughts and the same feelings; love one another as brothers, and be kind and humble with one another. Do not pay back evil with evil or cursing with cursing; instead pay back with a blessing . . . [you] must no longer speak evil, and must stop telling lies. . . . Turn away from evil and do good . . . seek peace and pursue it. For the Lord keeps His eyes on the righteous and always listens to their prayers; but He turns against those who do evil."

Reading: Matthew 5:20-24

But now I tell you: whoever is angry with his brother
will be brought before the judge. (Matthew 5:22)

Don't Make It a Mad, Mad, Mad World

A few years ago there was a song that everybody
was hearing, "It Takes Two to Tango." The tango is
a dance for two people, so you can't do that dance all
by yourself. But long before that dance somebody
said, "It takes two to make a fight." We never fight
ourselves. And we don't get mad at ourselves, either.
We always get mad at somebody else.

Our Lord told us it is wrong to get mad or angry.
He said it isn't wrong just to kill someone or get in a
fight with him, but even to get mad at someone else
is bad. Why is it wrong? Jesus told us that too: because
we are supposed to *love* our neighbor, not hate him.
But if we keep getting mad at somebody, we will hate
him after a while. And if we hate someone, we will
fight with him. And if we fight with him, we may hurt
him or even kill him.

Now, do you think killing and fighting and hating
is good? Does it make people happy or help them? Is
it *fun* to hate and fight? Even if God didn't tell us, we
would know that these things are no good. But besides,
He *did* tell us. He said, "You shall not kill." He said,
"Love your neighbor." And He said everyone who is
angry with his brother will be punished.

You *know* it is wrong to do these things. You wouldn't argue with me and say, "It isn't wrong. It's beautiful to get mad at people." Then, why do we get mad?

We get mad because we forget it is bad. Suppose someone does something or says something you don't like. What good does it do to get mad? Does it help the other fellow for you to holler and curse and swear at him? No! It only makes him worse. Does it help you? No! It makes you worse too. It makes you feel terrible, and it fills your heart, not with happiness but with sin. Does it make God happy? No! He is not happy with us at all when we get mad. So it doesn't do anybody any good when we get angry.

How can we keep from getting mad? Remember three things: First, it's bad to get mad; second, God doesn't want us to get mad; third, always try to be nice to other people. Don't just say, "I won't get mad." Say, "I am going to be nice to people." Jesus will help you to love others. Don't forget, it takes two to make a fight. Even if someone else is mad at you, he won't have anyone to fight with if you don't get mad at him.

Reading: Psalm 48

The Lord is great and must be highly praised in the city of our God, on His sacred mountain. (Psalm 48:1)

God Is "The Greatest"

What does "great" mean? Well, if it's a great day, it means nice. If you are in a great crowd, it means big. When you have a great way to go, it means long, and when you meet a great man, it means smart. "Great" really means a lot of different things.

When we say that *God* is great, it means all those things at once, because God is "nice" and "big" and "smart." Everything good that we can say, we can say about God. But when we say that God is great, it means *more* than it means when we say that anyone or anything else is great.

Nowadays people say that anybody or anything they like is not just great, but "the greatest." And that is something that we can really mean when we say it about God, because *He* really *is* "The Greatest."

God is everywhere; He knows everything and can do everything. God made everything and takes care of everything. God always was and always will be. Everyone and everything needs God's help, but He does not need anyone's help. We could go on and on saying "great" things about God to show that He is really "The Greatest."

But there is one single word that says all these things, a word we can use only for God and a word we use many times about Him. That word is "almighty." Sometimes we even call God "*The* Almighty." It really means "all-powerful" or "full of power." It means that God and only God is "The Greatest."

St. Paul tells us again that this almighty God, this God who is so great, is our loving Father. We are all children of the greatest Father of all, a Father who is full of power and goodness and love, a Father who is full of every good thing. How lucky we are to be the children of an almighty Father! No matter what happens, we should always feel safe and happy because we believe in God, the Father almighty. That is what we say in the Creed every Sunday. Say it whenever you have troubles or feel bad. Whenever things go wrong, just remember that the Lord is great and say, "I believe in God, the Father almighty."

Reading: Luke 19:41-48

If you only knew today what is needed for peace! [If you only knew what is good for you!] (Luke 19:42)

God Knows
What Is Good for You

How many of you would like to have this? Everyone, I guess, because it looks like a nice bottle of Cola — and that would be good on a nice warm day like this. But no matter how much you ask me, I would never give it to you, because I know it is *not* good for you. I keep my bug killer in this bottle. And even though you are not a bug, this stuff would kill you too if you drank it.

But I do not want you to get killed. So even if you get down on your hands and knees, I will not let you drink this. You might ask for it because you think it is good—but I would not give it to you because I know it is bad for you. You see the difference: You *think* it is good—I *know* it is bad.

Now, should you grumble if I don't give you something that will hurt you? You say, "No." But don't we grumble when God doesn't give us everything we ask for? St. Paul tells us that we should not grumble and that we should not test the Lord by asking for bad things. When I tell you the stuff in this bottle is bad for you, are you going to keep on asking me for it, so you can take a drink to see if it will kill you? That would be·crazy, wouldn't it? But don't we do that with God when we pray? Don't we say, "I want it—no matter what *You* say"? And if we don't get what we ask for, don't we grumble and complain that God isn't listening and that He doesn't answer our prayers?

But listen to what Jesus tells us today: "If you only knew what is good for you," He says. But we don't know what is good for us. He does, because He is God. Don't you think you can leave it up to Him? He is our best Friend. Don't you think He will give us what is best for us?

That's the way we should pray—by asking God

what is best for us. When you want something, tell God you are going to leave it up to Him. Tell Him you want it if He wants it too. Tell Him you *think* it's good, but remember, He *knows* if it's good. We ask God to hear all who pray to Him. And we hope that all who pray to Him will ask *only* for what *He* knows is good—because that's the way to get our prayers answered.

Reading: Psalm 65

To You we owe our hymn of praise, O God. (Psalm 65:1)

Whatever You Have
Is from God

"Anything you can do, I can do better." I wonder if you ever heard that song. It is supposed to be a joke. But some people sing that song all the time, and they really mean it. Or did you ever hear about the fellow who broke his arm patting himself on the back? That is supposed to be a joke too. But there are people who do pat themselves on the back all the time. Sometimes we call them "smart alecks" or "know-it-alls," people who are always bragging about themselves.

Nobody likes a "smart aleck" or a "know-it-all." Even God Himself tells us that bragging is no good. In the story of the Pharisee and the publican our Lord draws a picture of two men who pray. One of them is a smart aleck who says, "Thank God I'm not like other people. I'm a real good guy." But the other one asks God to help him because he is a poor, weak sinner. And then our Lord says that He will surely bless one of those two men, but not the other. You know the one He will bless — not the smart aleck, not the one who does the bragging, but the one who doesn't think much of himself. God is telling us that He will "pat us on the back" as long as we don't pat ourselves on the back.

Now, of course, everyone has some good things about him. Some people are good looking, some are strong, some are smart. Some people can sing, some can dance, and some can blow a bugle. Some people can do things better or quicker or easier than others. Some behave better or pray better or go to church more than others. But they spoil everything if they brag about it. As soon as they start "blowing their own horn" or singing, "Anything you can do, I can do better," the music turns sour.

The thing we all have to remember is what St. Paul tells us: Whatever good we have is a gift that God has given us. *He* is the One we should praise for whatever we have and whatever we can do — not ourselves. That is why we say, "To You we own our hymn of praise." If there is any good in us, it comes from God, not from ourselves. What comes from ourselves is the bad that is in us. If we admit that, we will be smart like the second man in the story. But if we pat ourselves on the back, we will be like the first fellow — just a smart *aleck*.

Reading: Mark 7:31-37

Then Jesus looked up to heaven, gave a deep groan, and said to the man, *Ephphatha,* which means, "Open up!" (Mark 7:34)

Use Your Mouth
and Your Ears

What in the world does that mean? *Ephphatha* is the word which Jesus speaks to the deaf and dumb man in today's Gospel story. And it is the word which was said to every one of us by the one who baptized us. But what does it mean? Well, St. Mark tells us right in the story: it means, "Open up!"

It's like this: if you want to get the soda pop out of this bottle, what do you have to do first? Open it, of course. And if you want to fill a jug with water, the first thing you have to do is take the cork out. Nothing can go in *or* out when an opening is plugged up.

The deaf and dumb man could not hear anything and could not say anything until his mouth and ears were opened. Our Lord did one of those wonderful things called a miracle so that fellow could hear and speak. He did a wonderful thing like that for each one of us on the day of our baptism, too.

Were we all deaf and dumb? Well, in a way, yes. You know that we were not God's friends when we were born. You might say we could not hear God and would not speak to Him. We were spiritually "deaf and dumb"—our souls could not "hear and speak." Then we were baptized. That gave us the wonderful gift of faith. It made us God's friends. The one who baptized us said, "Open up!" and then we could hear God and speak to Him—from then on we were one of the "faithful," a believer.

That's what faith is: having the "ears" of our soul open so we can hear what God says and having the "mouth" of our soul open so we can speak to Him. God did this wonderful thing for us when we were baptized. He gave us the great gift of faith.

Are the mouth and ears of your soul still open? We can plug up our ears and not listen; we can clamp our mouth shut if we want to. That is why we ask God to help us listen to Him better, so He will help us speak to Him more. Thank God that we are not deaf and dumb. Thank God that our souls are not "deaf and dumb," either, because Baptism made us able to hear God and speak to Him. May God help us always to have our mouth and ears open to Him, to listen better and say more—to God.

Reading: Luke 10:23-37

But the teacher of the Law wanted to put himself in the right, so he asked Jesus, "Who is my neighbor?" (Luke 10:29)

Everybody Is Your Neighbor

Once upon a time there were two countries that did not get along very well together. In fact the two countries were enemies. Those who lived in one country were Jews, and those who lived in the other were called Samaritans. One day one of the Jews was walking along a country road, and some bandits jumped him, beat him up, robbed him, and left him half dead in the ditch. In a little while a Samaritan came along and saw the dying Jew. Right away he stopped and helped the poor fellow. He bandaged him up, took him to a hotel, and paid for his care.

Why? Why did the Samaritan bother to help the Jew? He could have said: "He's a Jew; I don't like Jews; Jews and Samaritans are enemies, so I am not going to get mixed up with him." But that is not what he said. The Gospel tells us that "he was moved to pity at the sight." "The sight" was what he saw. And what he saw was a poor, suffering man; he saw another human being; he saw a person like himself; he saw one of God's people. He did not see a rock or a log, a cat or a dog; he did not see a Jew or an enemy. He saw a person.

He could not feel sorry for a rock or a log; he could

not love a cat or a dog; he might not want to help a Jew or an enemy. But he could feel sorry for another person: he could love one of God's people; he could want to help another human being. That is what made the Jew a neighbor to the Samaritan. Rocks and logs, cats and dogs are not our neighbors — but people are. And God tells us we must love our neighbors because they are people. It did not matter what the poor fellow in the ditch was like. The Samaritan helped him because he was his neighbor.

Jesus told that story, and He told it for just one reason: to show us that all people are our neighbors and that we should love them. It doesn't matter what they are like. It doesn't matter what they do or what color they are. It doesn't matter where they are from or what they have done to us. If we want to be like our heavenly Father, we have to be Good Samaritans. Jesus Himself said so: "Go and act like him."

Reading: Galatians 3:15-22

. . . so that those who believe might receive the promised gift that is given on the basis of faith in Jesus Christ. (Galatians 3:22)

God Promises — We Believe

I think you have all heard of the Promised Land. Thousands of years ago God promised a man named Abraham that He would give him and all of his children a special country to live in. And God did give them that land. He kept His promise because Abraham and his children believed what God told them. The land God gave His people is called the Holy Land now, because it is the place where Jesus was born and lived and died.

And who was Jesus? Jesus was the Promised One—the Savior whom God promised to send into the world long before He promised a country to Abraham. And what did Jesus do? He promised something too; He promised an everlasting homeland to all of us, a place we usually call heaven, but which is also sometimes called the "Promised Land."

God the Father promised His people a place to live their earthly lives for a few years. God the Son promises His people a place to live their heavenly lives forever. God the Father kept His promise, and God the Son will keep His promise too.

Is that all? Is everything up to God? Does He just promise everything to everybody and then give it to them? Oh, no! Today we learn that God gives His promise to those who believe. Our Lord told a sick man He had cured: "Your faith has saved you." He promised to heal the man, and He did—because the man *believed*. In the prayer today we ask God: "Make us love what You have commanded so that we may get what You have promised." God promised us heaven, but He will give it only to those who believe in Him enough to do what He wants. And the apostle tells us right out that "those who believe [will] receive the promised gift."

93

Who got into the Promised Land? Those who believed in Jesus. Who are saved by the Promised One? Those who believe in Him. Who will get to the Promised Land of heaven? Those who believe, those who have faith. God has made His promise to all of us. But He cannot keep His promise unless we believe. That is why our prayer today starts out with the words: "Almighty and eternal God, deepen our faith." We do believe, Lord; help us to believe more and more.

Reading: Matthew 6:24-33

Look at the birds flying around. (Matthew 6:26)

Leave Everything Up to God

It always makes us happy every spring when we hear the song of the first robin. We all look out the window as soon as we hear it. Wouldn't you be surprised when you looked for that first robin to see him with a lunch box on his wing trudging off to work, going out to the farm to plant the crops? That would be funny, wouldn't it? But what do you see when you spy the first robin? You see him hopping happily across the lawn without a care in the world. Once in a while he stops to pull a worm out of the ground. He doesn't worry about his dinner. He knows the worms will always be there.

But you and I worry, don't we? When a friend doesn't visit you, if you don't get a present, because you haven't got new shoes, as soon as you have a headache, what do you do? Worry and complain.

And what does God want us to do? He wants us to trust in Him. That is why Jesus told the story about the birds and the flowers. He showed us how the Father takes care of them. The birds always have enough to eat, the flowers are always growing and healthy, and they don't have to worry a bit.

Now what does God think more of: you or a robin, you or a lily? Why, you, of course. Jesus said we are worth a lot more than birds and flowers. So God surely will take better care of us than He does of them.

Our Lord says, "Don't worry about what you are going to eat or drink or wear." Don't complain about the headache or the shoes or the present or the friend. What *should* we do? Jesus says, "Worry about getting to heaven and being good." That's what really counts. God knows when you have a headache, He knows when you need new shoes or want a present or a friend, and God will take care of it — IF you leave it up to Him.

If we are doing what God wants, if we are trying to be good and want to be in God's family, then God will take care of everything else. Try to think of that every time you see a bird or a flower. God takes care of *them.* He takes much better care of *us.* Leave everything up to Him, and you can be as happy-go-lucky as the robin in spring.

Jesus said, "Young man! Get up, I tell you!" (Luke 7:14)

Faith Makes Life Easier

"Oh, my aching back!" Backache, headache, toothache! Cuts and burns and broken toes; bumps and bangs and bloody nose! What a beating we take! Always something going wrong with these bodies of ours. Always something to make us feel bad. Always something to make us moan and groan.

Wouldn't it be wonderful if we could just be without a single ache or pain for a while? Well, do you know that we can? Do you know that our bodies can be strong and well and healthy, not just for a while but forever? Do you know that we can live on and on and on without any sickness and without ever hurting the least bit? Of course you know it, because you say it every time you say the Creed: "I look for the resurrection of the dead."

When you say those words, you are saying you believe your body will come back to life someday. You believe it because you heard that "the dead man sat up and began to speak" after our Lord said to him, "Young man! Get up, I tell you!" And you believe God will say that to you someday too.

That is part of the "faith" we have been talking about, one of the things we say we believe every Sunday in the Creed. But what does that have to do with our aching back, our bloody nose, or our broken toes? It has a lot to do with it, because when our bodies come back to life, they will never be able to suffer or die again.

When we say we believe in the resurrection of the body, we are saying all that: there will be no more aches and pains, no more sickness and death. This is what we believe, and this is how our faith, our belief in the resurrection of the dead, can help us right here and now.

Instead of saying, "Oh, my aching back," the next time try saying, "I await the resurrection of the dead." If we remember that Jesus will bring our bodies back to a life of no aches and pains, it will be easier to put up with every pain in the back we have while we're waiting.

Reading: Luke 14:1-14

A man whose legs and arms were swollen came to Jesus. (Luke 14:2)

All People Are God's People

I am going to do a lot of writing; so I have a big bunch of nice new pencils ready. Oh, oh, here's one that's broken! It has no point. Well, I might as well throw it away. Is that what we do with a pencil that has a broken point? Of course not! We don't throw it away. We sharpen it, and then it's just as good as the other pencils.

The crippled man in today's Gospel story was like a broken pencil. But you notice that our Lord did not throw him out. He took the man and healed him. And you notice that Jesus did not stay away from the meal just because there were cripples there. He never stayed away, no matter what kind of people were there. We see our Lord with good and bad people, strong and weak people, black and white people, healthy and crippled people. And Jesus loved them all because they were people – God's people.

Remember, the Son of God came down from heaven to be with His people on earth. He came to *be* one of God's people. And He came to show those people how to act. He wants *us* to be like Him, to do what He did, to act the way He did.

Do we? Do we treat people around us the way Jesus did? Or do we stay away from some people because of the way they talk or look? Do we want to throw some people out because they are sick or crippled?

We come to church on Sunday to show that we love God. But remember we do *not* love God if we do not love God's *people* – all of them, no matter who they are or what they are. If we think we are better than someone else, if we have a grudge against another person, if we hate somebody, then we are certainly not doing what our Lord did.

He never stayed away from anyone. If they were sinners or sick or crippled, He did not throw them out. He even did something very special for them: He took their sins or their sickness away, He healed them and cured them – because He loved them.

We may not be able to change people the way Jesus did, but we can love them the way He did. Remember to tell Him: "You, O Lord, are good and forgiving, [full of] kindness to all," and then ask Him to help *you* to be good and forgiving and full of kindness to *all.*

Reading: Ephesians 4:1-6

There is one God and Father of all men, who is Lord of all, works through all, and is in all. (Ephesians 4:6)

True Faith Means Brotherly Love

"I love me!" Did you ever say that to anyone when he was "patting himself on the back"? Did you ever think that it is wrong for people to love themselves? Well, it is wrong—if we love ourselves *too much.* But, believe it or not, God *wants* us to love ourselves. Did you know that Jesus said, "You shall love your neighbor *as yourself"?* Well, if we have to love other people the way we love ourselves, then we must have to love ourselves first.

But the whole point is that we must love other people just as much as we love ourselves. Do you want yourself to get hurt, to be sick, to have troubles, to get killed, to go to hell? Of course not! Then, our Lord says, you must not want these things to happen to other people, either. Do you want nice things for yourself, do you want to be happy, do you want to be God's friend, do you want to get to heaven? Of course! Then, says our Lord, you must want these good things for your neighbor too.

That's what it means to love our neighbor as we love ourselves. It does not mean that we have to fall "head over heels in love" with everybody. It does not mean that we have to like everything everybody does. It does not mean that we have to be "crazy" over the other fellow.

Loving our neighbor just means being nice to other people; it means being good to the other fellow. We are all "good" to ourselves—and that's how we should be with everyone else.

Why? St. Paul tells us why: because we are all one big family, we are all children of one heavenly Father, we are all together because we have all been baptized and all believe the same things. If we tear the family of God apart, it is like tearing ourselves apart. But we do *not* tear ourselves apart, because we love ourselves. If we tear the family of God apart, we are not loving our neighbor as ourselves.

You remember, we said that true faith, really believing, means doing what God wants. God wants us to be one big, happy family. If we really believe, we will try to be one big, happy family by loving ourselves and loving our neighbor as ourselves. Then it will mean something when we say: "There is one God and Father of all men, who is Lord of all, works through all, and is in all."

Reading: Matthew 9:1-8

Is it easier to say, "Your sins are forgiven," or to say, "Get up and walk"? (Matthew 9:5)

Jesus Has Power
to Forgive You

When you look at this electric lamp, can you tell if there is any electric power in it? Not really, not just by looking at it, not even if there were a bulb in it, and not even if you could see that it is plugged in. Well, how *can* you find out if there is power in it? Three ways: First, by having me *tell* you that there is electricity in the lamp. But if you don't believe me, then there is a second way: You could come up and stick your finger in the socket. But that is *not* the way to find out—because you might get hurt. If the power *is* on, you would get a terrible shock. So the *best* way to find out is to put a *bulb* in the socket. There! Now you see the light, and you know that electricity is coming through into the bulb.

When people looked at Jesus, they could not tell if there was any special power in Him either—not just by looking at Him. But Jesus *told* people that He had the power of God—the power to take away sins. You heard Him say that today when He told the sick man, "Your sins are forgiven." But the people looking at Him did not believe it—because they could not *see* that power any more than you can see the electric power in this lamp when the bulb is out.

But then our Lord did something that they *could* see: He made the crippled man well; He took his sickness away; He used His power to make him able to walk. It was like turning on a light. When they saw the poor cripple get up and walk, then they knew that Jesus had the power of God—just as you knew there was power in this lamp when you saw the light.

I hope that you and I take our Lord's word for it when He says He has the power to take away our sins. I hope we do not tell Him that He has to prove it to us. Instead, let's tell Him that we believe Him and thank Him for using His wonderful power to make us His friends again whenever we have sinned.

Reading: Ephesians 4:23-32

Do not give the devil a chance. (Ephesians 4:27)

Watch Out for the Devil!

Today I am going to tell you a story about a camel. This camel had carried his master across the desert all day, and now he was resting next to his master's tent. Soon it began to get chilly, and the camel was cold. He stuck his nose inside the tent. It was nice and warm. But his driver said, "Get out!" "Just my nose," said the camel, "it's cold out here." "Well, all right, just your nose," said the man and went back to sleep. Pretty soon the camel had his whole head in the tent. "Just my head," he said when the driver tried to put him out. But the man gave in again and let the camel keep his head in the tent. Then it was "Just my neck" and "Just my shoulders." And then, do you know what happened? All of a sudden the camel was in the tent and the man was out in the cold.

St. Paul tells us today that we must not be like the camel driver: "Do not give the devil a chance." We must not let the devil even get his nose into our lives. When we were baptized, it was like putting on a beautiful, clean robe, the goodness of God. Now the devil keeps trying to push us out—not out of a tent but out of that white robe, out of God's grace. He is always trying to get his nose in by getting us to tell just a little lie or steal just a little something or just get a little mad. But St. Paul says we must not lie at all or get angry or steal even a little bit, because those are the openings through which the devil gets into our lives. And once he gets in, then he keeps pushing and pushing us to do wrong until he pushes us right away from God, right out of the beautiful white robe of God's grace that we got in Baptism.

And our Lord shows us in the story about the wedding what happens if we do not have His grace. The man who was not dressed the right way for the wedding banquet was thrown out. And if we do not have the beautiful robe of grace on our souls, we will be "thrown out" of heaven too.

God made us good when we were baptized. But we have to *stay* good. We have to keep the devil out of our lives by trying not to do even little things that are wrong. Remember, little sins lead to big sins, and this keeps us out of heaven. And remember the camel. His driver let him put just his nose in the tent at first, but pretty soon the driver was out in the cold. "Do not give the devil a chance," if you do not want to be "put out" of heaven.

Reading: John 4:46-53

The man believed Jesus' words and went. (John 4:50)

You Can Believe God's Word

I have two little (!) books here. I wonder if you know what they are. This one is a dictionary. The other one is a Bible. Both of them are full of words. The dictionary is full of words that people use. The Bible is full of words that God uses to His people. I believe what is in the dictionary. And I believe what is in the Bible. So, what is the difference?

Well, let's take a look at what happened to the man in today's Gospel story. His little boy was dying, so he asked Jesus to make him better. Our Lord told the man that his son would not die, and the man took His word for it. By the time he got back home, the boy was all better. Because that man believed the Word of God, one of those wonderful things called a miracle happened, and his son's life was saved.

Now, you know that there won't be any miracles if I believe what is in this dictionary. But will there be miracles if I believe in the Bible? Maybe not. But wonderful things happen when we believe in this Book, because it is the Word of God. The most wonderful thing of all is that we become a better friend of God the more we listen to and believe in His Word.

Every time we come to church we are hearing the Word of God. The whole first part of the service is called the Liturgy of the Word, because in the Epistle and the Gospel and the sermon God's Word is coming to us. What we hear there is right out of the Bible. The better we listen and believe what we hear, the closer it will bring us to God. The dictionary can tell us what to say to God, but the Bible tells us what God says to us.

St. Paul tells us not to be fools, but to make the most of every chance we have to be better followers of the Lord. Every time we come to church we have that chance by listening to God's Word and believing it. If we put our trust in the word Jesus has spoken, like the father of the dying boy, something wonderful will happen to us, too.

Reading: Matthew 18:21-35

The master felt sorry for him, so he forgave him the debt and let him go. . . . And he sent the servant to jail to be punished. (Matthew 18:27, 34)

Forgive as You Are Forgiven

Nobody likes two-faced people. They are the kind of people who are nice to you while you are looking at them, but turn against you the minute you turn your back. But did you notice the king in today's story? He was nice to his servant one minute and mad at him the next. Do you think the king was two-faced? Do you think he double-crossed his servant?

Well, let's take a good look at him. Why was he nice? Because he felt sorry for a poor fellow who couldn't pay back some money he borrowed. And why was he mad? Because the same fellow was not nice to someone who owed *him* some money. The king was glad to forgive his servant, but he was angry when his servant would not forgive someone else. Do you think the king was wrong? I guess not!

In fact, our Lord tells us that this is just the way God is with us. God is good to us, and He expects us to be good to others. How many times God has forgiven us! How many times He has taken us back after we have run away from Him! And what about us? How many times we hold a grudge against other people! How many times we will not forgive those who hurt us! How many times we want to get even with others!

That's what we call double-crossing. *That* is really being two-faced. *We* are the ones in the wrong. We are the ones who keep saying, "Forgive us our trespasses as we forgive those who trespass against us." We are the ones who keep promising that we will be good to other people because God has been so good to us. Let's stop being two-faced. Let's start looking at God's people with the same face that we use to look to God. Let's begin to forgive other people the way God has been forgiving us.

Reading: Mark 7:14-23

This people pays Me lip service, but their heart is far from Me. (Mark 7:6)

Clean Inside and Outside

When my boy brought in the newspaper this morning, look what happened! He had dirty hands. Well, I don't like my newspaper dirty, but it *is* only a newspaper, and it cost only a few cents — so I didn't scold him very hard. But look at *this:* a beautiful Bible! Now, he should get a real scolding (shouldn't he?) because this is a special book, and it cost lots of money. You see, there is a difference: dirt can be very bad in one place and not so bad in another.

Jesus tells us that in today's Gospel story. Some smart alecks said it was terrible that the apostles didn't wash their hands before eating. Well, we *should* wash our hands before we eat. *But* it is not a *sin* if we don't. And that's what the smart alecks were saying. They were trying to make it look as though the apostles had done something really bad by eating with dirty hands. That would be like saying that the dirt on this newspaper is a sin.

And what did our Lord do? He scolded the smarties — but not his apostles. He said, "You make a big deal out of dirty hands. But dirt on your hands is not so bad. The thing that's really bad is sin in your heart. Keeping your hands clean will never get you to heaven. What you have to do is keep your soul clean.

A little mud or grease or dirt will never keep you out of heaven. Bad thoughts and words and deeds will."

It's something like getting the newspaper and the Bible dirty. Now, of course, even these finger marks on the costly Bible are not a sin. But they *are* much worse than the finger marks on the newspaper. But no matter how clean you keep the newspaper and the Bible, it's no good if your *soul* isn't clean. That's when Jesus would say, "This people pays Me lip service, but their heart is far from Me." They *say* they love Me, but they don't act that way.

We cannot fool God. We can come here to church every Sunday and *say* we love Him. But if we sin all week long, if we think and say and do the things God doesn't like Monday, Tuesday, Wednesday, Thursday, Friday, and Saturday, and then come back and look real holy again on Sunday, our hearts are really far from Him. Then we are just being smarties and phonies. That's like being very careful of an old newspaper and getting a beautiful Bible all dirty.

Don't try to fool God by just looking clean on the outside. Remember, He knows what is in your mind and heart and soul. Be sure you keep *those* clean — not just your hands. Remember what we said so many times today: "He who *does* good will live in the presence of the Lord."

Reading: Mark 8:31-38

If anyone wants to come with Me . . . he must forget himself, carry his cross, and follow Me. (Mark 8:34)

Sadness Before Happiness

This baseball makes us all think of the World Series. Pretty soon everyone will be watching them hitting home runs in the biggest games of the year. And how does that make everybody feel? Happy! Right! Everyone hollers and shouts for joy. And the fellow who wallops the ball over the fence really feels good, doesn't he?

But if I were out there, *this* is what would happen: Strike one! strike two! strike three! and you're out at the old ball game. I couldn't hit a home run if you paid me. But neither could Babe Ruth or Mickey Mantle the first time they ever picked up a baseball bat. It takes a lot of practice for any player to get to be a great hitter. The home-run kings had the sadness of striking out more than once before they could have the happiness of hitting home runs.

That is what Jesus is telling us in today's Gospel story: If you want happiness, you have to have sadness, too. That's the way it was with Him. He said He would have to suffer much, be hated by people, and be killed — all that sadness first — and *then* come back to life with the happiness of Easter Sunday.

Well, that didn't sound good at all to Peter, so he took our Lord aside and scolded Him. He said to Jesus,

"You can't let all those awful things happen to You. We won't let You have all that sadness. We're going to keep things nice and easy for You." And then Jesus scolded *him*. He even called Peter a devil because he was trying to make things too easy for Him.

That is when our Lord said: "If anyone wants to come with Me . . . he must . . . follow Me." If you want to follow Jesus to the happiness of heaven, you have to have the sadness of striking out, too.

Life on earth was *not* a bowl of cherries, it was *not* a bed of roses for our Lord. And it isn't for us, either. We all have our troubles, we all have hard times. Things sometimes go wrong for all of us. But that is part of the game of life — just as strikeouts are part of the game of baseball. You can't be a home-run king without some sadness. And you can't go home with Christ the King without some sadness.

So the next time things go wrong with you, don't gripe and growl and grumble. Think of Babe Ruth or Mickey Mantle striking out. Think of Jesus hanging on the cross. Then remember: after all the troubles and heartaches and sadness and strikeouts here on earth you will enjoy the happiness of home runs and heaven.

Where is your courage? How little faith you have! (Matthew 8:26)

God Always Takes Care of Us

Can you see what this is? Yes, an egg. And where did it come from? Right—a chicken. I didn't have a chicken handy, so I brought the egg. You all know what a chicken is. But what I really want to know is what you mean when you call a boy or a girl "chicken." You mean they are afraid. When I was a little boy, we called scared kids "fraidy cats." Now they call them "chicken." Jesus really called the apostles cowards, for they had lost courage. It means the same thing.

The apostles were afraid, scared to death, because they thought the boat they were in was going to sink in that terrible storm. Jesus was right in the same boat, but He was asleep. The apostles were "chicken," so they yelled for help. They woke our Lord up and said, "Lord, save us! We are going to drown." And the first thing Jesus said was, "Where is your courage?" Today He might say, "How come you are so chicken?" Why are you afraid?

But did you notice that our Lord did not wait for the apostles to answer Him. He answered the question Himself. He told them why they were afraid. "How little faith you have!" He said. And isn't that exactly what's wrong with us a lot of times? Aren't we cowards, aren't we afraid, aren't we "chicken" because we have such weak faith? If we really believed in God as we should, we would never worry and fret and stew about things, because we would know that God takes care of everything. If our faith is strong, we know how much God loves us, and we are not afraid.

Do you remember God saying to us: "Call upon Me and I will hear you," and, "Whatever you ask for . . . believe . . . and it shall be done to you."

Sometimes it seems as though God is asleep. Jesus was sleeping because He is not only God but man, too, and His body needed sleep just as ours does. But you know that God Himself does not need sleep. If we call Him, He will surely hear us. If we believe in Him, He will surely answer us. And as long as He hears and answers, there is no reason for us to be "chicken." But, remember, we have to do the calling and the believing.

Reading: John 18:33-38

My kingdom does not belong to this world. (John 18:36)

The King of Love

Here you see a gold crown. What kind of people wear gold crowns? Yes, kings—and queens. Well, I guess I'll try it on. So! Am I a king? Of course not—a crown doesn't make anybody a king.

Well, what does make a person a king? What is a king, anyhow? A ruler of a country; the one who is in charge of all the people. And we call the king's country and his people "his kingdom." The people in his kingdom have to obey the king and do what he says. They might even hate the fellow, and he might be a terrible king — but he's the boss, and everyone has to do as he says. He isn't king just when he wears his crown, because that isn't what makes him the ruler. He is king because he has the *power* to rule over his kingdom.

Now, what about Jesus? He said that He is a king: Christ the King. Does He need a crown to be king? No! All He needs is the power to rule over His people. But Jesus is God; so we know He has the power. He is the most powerful King of all — and He *is* King of *all,* because He has power over every man, woman, and child in the whole world. The world is His kingdom — and all the people in the world belong to the kingdom of Christ.

But Jesus said, "My kingdom does not belong to this world." Well, what in the world "world" does it belong to? You know that: the *next* world, the *other* world. It is not an earthly kingdom, but the kingdom of heaven. Christ is not an earthly king, but our heavenly King. But most of all He is the King of love.

Some earthly kings use only power to rule their people. If they do not obey, the king has them beaten or thrown into prison or killed. But look at Jesus. He *does* have a crown, but it is a crown of thorns. He *does* have a throne, but it is the throne of the cross. Our King *doesn't* have *us* beaten. *He* was beaten for *us.* That beating and that throne and that crown do not show His power over us. They show His love for us.

Sometimes people obey their earthly kings because they are terrible men and they are afraid of them. But our heavenly King is a King of love. Because Christ our King is the King of love, let's tell Him that we are going to do what He wants because *we* love *Him*.

Reading: Psalm 136

"Give thanks to the Lord, for He is good." (Psalm 136:1)

Thanksgiving and Giving Thanks

If I give you this great big dish of chocolate ice cream, what will you say? "Thank you," of course. And if I won't *let* you have this ice cream, because I know it is filled with poison that will kill you, what should you do? You should still thank me, shouldn't you? Or if you are sick and I give you a spoonful of very bitter medicine because I know it will make you better, you will thank me, too.

Now, you don't like the bitter medicine at all. And you don't like it when I keep the beautiful-looking ice cream from you, either. But you know I am your friend, and you know that everything I do is for your own good. So you thank me even when you don't "like" the things I do to you.

God gives us a lot of things that we want and things that we like — like chocolate ice cream. When He gives us those things, it is easy to thank Him. But sometimes He gives us things we don't like — like the bitter medicine. And other times He does *not* give us what we want — like the poison ice cream.

Every year on Thanksgiving Day we all stop to thank God. But we should thank Him *every* day. We always thank God too, I hope, when He gives us the things we like and want. But we should thank Him also for all the other things He gives us — and even for the things He does not let us have.

Remember, God is our very best Friend. He gives us only what is good for us, and He will *not* give us what He knows will hurt us. Be sure you thank God for the bitter medicine He sometimes gives you to make you better. Be sure you thank Him for the things He *doesn't* give you to keep you from getting hurt.

At the end of our liturgy we say, "Thanks be to God." Say it at the end of every *day,* too. Whether God gives you good things or bitter things or keeps bad things away from you, remember He is doing it because He loves you. Be sure to thank Him for all of them. God helps us in many ways every day. Don't forget to say "Thanks be to God" every day.